Let's Do This Life Thing!

By: Angel Marie Renee' Mayes

Edited by: Tiffiany Collier

BK Royston Publishing LLC

Jeffersonville, IN

BK Royston Publishing
P. O. Box 4321
Jeffersonville, IN 47131
502-802-5385
http://bkroystonpublishing.com
bkroystonpublishing@gmail.com

© Copyright – 2016

Cover Illustration: Donna Ayers
Cover Format: Bill Lacy

ISBN-13: 978-0692734438

ISBN-10: 0692734430

Printed in the United States of America

Dedication

I dedicate this book to my two children,
Majesty Jeane' Mayes and **Major Jeromiah
Mayes**.

No matter what happens in life, always remember
Never give up!
I love you both with every fiber of my being!

Acknowledgement

As I begin to spread my wings yet further, I will first give Honor to God Almighty. I thank Him for allowing me to be born! I am so grateful for the blessings he purposely placed in my life.

I thank my biological mother (whom I do not know) for encapsulating me when I was catapulted to this earth. I am grateful for my foster family whom I know as the Lancasters from Shelbyville, Kentucky. Beyond measureable gratefulness is what I have for my mother, my REAL mother, the woman who raised me and taught me many valuable lessons about life and living, Betty Jean Mayes, and my earthly father, George Madison Mayes Jr.

I'm thankful for my two sister's Gabrielle Mayes and Dana Mayes and for their support. I give a very special shout out to my God Parents Vivien and Greg Ogburn for standing in the gap for my parents when needed.

I'm grateful for the Pastors and Spiritual leaders I have sat under; I have learned and grown with their guidance and teaching.

I must extend acknowledgements to a host of extended and non-blood family members for being my support system during those trying times and taboo subjects that only we could experience together, understand without judgement, and grow further into our own individualized, interdependent selves. I'm grateful for your support, listening ears, correction, and celebration concerning my endeavors in life! To name a few, A.E. Pettus, C.M. Dorsey, D.A. Link, Andrea Greer. The others of you know who you are and what you mean to me!

I hope and pray that my story elevates, evaluates, and encourages many to stay the course through struggle and triumphs and DO THIS LIFE THING!

Much Love!

Table of Contents

Introduction

This is my story. A real true to life testimony of my life thus far. When I was born my biological mother was incarcerated. At three days old I was in foster home in a small town not far from the city I was born in. After a short while of living in the foster home I was adopted by a single woman. Layers of life collected together before I could catch up with the realization that meandering through life is not an option for me. Through many experiences and mistakes, relationships, trials and tribulations I learn to become better and begin to heal from seen and unseen dangers by paying attention to life situations, making proactive choices, and experiencing life to the fullest. By learning to step out on Faith and look up for help, I develop into an interdependent young adult woman who is Doing This Life Thing!

Chapter 1
In the Beginning- Here I Am!

"The Lord is my shepherd; I shall not want." Psalm 23:1 KJV

On August 12, 1977 a little mixed baby was born to a single mother. She was pulled out of her mother's womb, cleaned up, then passed through her mother's arms, to the nurses' arms and then finally placed in her bed. Baby Hardy went from the Neonatal Unit of the University of Louisville Hospital, into the backseat of a car belonging to a Kentucky state social worker by the name of Ms. Relay, by which the infant traveled to the doorstep of Mr. and Mrs. Lancaster. This was her final destination at three days old, for now. The Lancaster foster home was a well-known foster care provider in Shelbyville, Kentucky. There were about seven other children who lived here with the couple, and Baby Hardy was welcomed with open arms.

"This baby is something special. She just a wee little thing, I think they said she was three days old when they brought her here. So this is her third day with us. Imma call her Angel. Yeah, that's what we'll call her."

Mrs. Lancaster held her up in the air as she looked into her twinkling eyes. The baby's feet dangled and her arms flailed in excitement, responding to the gazes of her newfound family. There were Michael, James, Richard, Selena, Jared, Layla, and Brenden. The brothers and sisters cooed and chattered prompting a smile from the little Angel.

"Okay! That's enough now children! Let her rest for a while!" directed Mrs. Lancaster as she laid little Angel down on the couch. She placed a pillow beside the baby as she called out chores to the other children.

"Now you know Mr. Lancaster will be home soon! Layla, take the roast out, get that bread off the counter, and run it in the oven. James, you stir them greens up and turn them down on low. Jared and Selena, yall two set the table. Brenden, get the glasses down from the top shelf. And Michael, you and Richard fill 'em up with ice. Make sure yall have them place sets right, you know how Mr. Lancaster feels about his utensils bein' in the right place."

The family sat down at the dining table to await Mr. Lancaster's arrival. They all discussed who was gonna wash and change and feed and rock the baby to sleep.

"So long as I get the last kiss on her forehead before bedtime, I ain't worried 'bout nothin' else!" informed a determined Richard.

No sooner than he ended that sentence, the front door crept open revealing a staunch shouldered, stern faced

Mr. Lancaster. "Good evenin' family." he greeted them.

"Well good evenin' to you Mister." Mrs. Lancaster always responded to her husband first, before anyone else; she could always tell how his time at the factory had been by the way he looked at her when he answered back. "How was your day?"

Mr. Lancaster removed his brimmed hat from his head and sat it atop the coat rack that sat to the left of the front door. He looked across the living room and dining room and into the kitchen where Mrs. Lancaster stood in front of the stove with her head turned to face her husband. She caught a glimpse of the twinkle in his right eye, which always meant that he was smiling inside and just tired and hungry. On that note, she gave everyone else the cue to bombard "Daddy Lancaster" with love. All of the children scooted back from their seats and ran to wrap their arms around Mr. Lancaster. They just loved him. As everyone else took their seats, Layla and Mrs. Lancaster brought the dishes and platters of food to the table. Mrs. Lancaster turned to check the pot of water that had started to boil on the stove while Layla pulled the pitcher of sun tea from the refrigerator. Turning back to the table and passing Mrs. Lancaster's peripheral vision, Layla gave her a pleading look of excitement. She knew that Daddy Lancaster did not know about the new baby because of the sudden call from the state and the speedy drop-off by the social worker. Mrs. Lancaster returned the questioning look with an "I'll-give-him-the-news" nod and she turned to finish warming the baby's bottle.

The family bowed their heads for grace, which was led by Mr. Lancaster, and then they dug in to the made-for-Sunday dinner. They scooped out portions of greens, macaroni and cheese, sweet carrots, roast and potatoes, and sliced cornbread. The pitcher of tea was just beginning its route around the table when Mrs. Lancaster pulled her chair out to sit down. She casually sat the baby bottle filled with warm sweet milk and wrapped in a towel, on the corner of the table near the place where she sat and began to fill her plate with the delicacies that spread across the dining table.

Before Mrs. Lancaster took the first bite of food from her fork, Mr. Lancaster spoke in a subtle yet firm voice, "Now, mama, you know we've been living this life together long enough to know each other like the fronts and backs of our hands. So with that being said, what on God's green earth do you have a warm baby bottle sittin' on the corner of this table for?"

The corners of Mrs. Lancaster's lips turned up slightly towards her cheeks, she slightly blinked her eyes and took a slow, deep breath. She put her fork full of greens down onto the plate, and thought to herself *"This must be a really good baby 'cause she ain't made one sound. Not a coo or nothing'!"*

She touched Mr. Lancaster's elbow and gently nodded her head towards the living room. Immediately Mr. Lancaster saw the pillow on the edge of the couch. Although he knew that there was a baby on the other side of that bed pillow, he did not miss a bite or a sip while he sat at the head of the table.

Everyone waited in anticipation to see what his response was going to be. No one moved from the table, even though all plates and glasses had been cleaned. Mr. Lancaster clasped his hands together and rested his forehead on the knuckles of his index fingers. He sat that way for about two or three minutes. When he raised his head, he scooted back from his seat, went into the kitchen, and washed his hands. He turned and looked each family member in their eyes as he nodded his head upon each contact. Mr. Lancaster placed his hand upon Mrs. Lancaster's shoulder, picked up the warm baby bottle and walked into the living room to meet little Angel. When he stood at the front of the couch, he looked down on a fair-skinned child who gazed right back up at him.

Mrs. Lancaster prompted the children to go and get ready for bed. They all left the table. She sat there to finish her meal as Daddy Lancaster began to nurture the baby.

Days and weeks went by and the home of the Lancaster's just overflowed with love. All of the children had their specific special times with little Angel. Richard stuck by his agenda and always got the last kiss on her forehead before bedtime. Over time other children came to the Lancaster household. The family grew closer as time went by, although some of the members interchanged due to adoptions or reunions with biological families. Little Angel remained with the Lancasters for about two years, which seemed like a lifetime to the family. They loved her so. She was something very special. At one point, the Lancasters tried to adopt Angel but they had already exceeded the limit of adoptive children to remain a foster home as well. So, inevitably, eventually, Angel would be adopted into another family. No one knew when the day or the hour would come, but it did, and it came quicker than anyone thought.

I was born on August 12, 1977. My mother was in jail at the time. She had quite a bit of time to serve, so she couldn't keep me. Wow! I feel like I had watched other kids' lives before I came to earth. I feel like I had felt sorry for the kids who were teased because they were adopted and didn't look like their other family members. The feeling is unexplainable. I have tried to put it into words sometimes, but I guess I'll just have to show you the experiences I have had since the day I remember…

I was asleep on the couch in the living room of our two-bedroom apartment, mama and me that is. I could hear the T.V., I think…and I was dreaming. A witch was chasing me down the bank of a river. I ran and ran... When I finally tried to catch my breath behind a tree, I felt the witch grabbing me from behind, and when I jumped so hard from being startled, I woke myself up. "It's okay sweetheart." whispered a sweet consoling voice. "I'm here. It was just a bad dream."

I arose to look around and I finally brought my mind to my mama's and my apartment. I felt okay, I guess… but I remembered that was not the first time I had that dream when a witch was chasing me. There was another dream that I would have quite often where I would just start falling. I didn't know where from, but I would just find myself falling….

That is the first day that I remember knowing I was real. I was a human being. For some reason, even though I knew that I was a real human being, I didn't always feel like it. Sometimes I felt like an invisible shiny person. How does that work? I don't really know, but that is the way I often felt. That was on the outside. On the inside I felt like a big open space filled with supernatural stuff; only I could not control any of it. Whatever the stuff was inside of me, it did whatever it wanted to do whenever it chose to do so. I always felt funny…kind of out of sorts, or lost. Even though I was surrounded by loving people, this tangible world felt so vast and the intangible world, with which I had many encounters, felt even more vast! It seemed like I was just floating through the days and nights.

I was about five, I think, when I started to feel my way around these unfamiliar places. But no sooner than I reached out my hand to explore my surroundings, my surroundings moved around and cajoled into another kind of substance. I still could not catch up with myself inside or out. What's going on? How does this work?

As I pressed myself to find stable ground on which to walk on and an open sky in which to fly, life became more familiar to me. Every day I felt a little more human. I guess it was all a part of growing from a toddler into childhood age. I didn't know. All I knew was that a lot of what I was experiencing was interesting, so I just kept on allowing myself to feel my way through; for the most part.

Every now and then I would go into the secret capsule inside of that big space inside of me and twirl around in circles again and again. It wasn't voluntary though. I just went sometimes. Like a caterpillar prepares to transfigure into a new form of life, I would go into my cocoon time and time again. Unlike the caterpillar, I never stayed enclosed long enough to transfigure. I still, somehow, always felt out of place wherever I went.

Angel Marie Renee' Mayes

Chapter 2
I Wonder if We Played Baseball

Have you ever felt abandoned without really being abandoned? Well, abandoned means to be abruptly left; suddenly let go of; cast aside, deserted and left behind amongst many other descriptions. It has different emotional consequences depending on which side of it you are standing. If you are the abandoner, there could probably be feelings of resentment, relief, guilt, or uneasiness. On the other hand, if you are the abandonee, then you will have feelings of fear, disappointment, anger, and confusion. Either way, abandonment is not a pleasurable experience.

We stood in the toy aisle of the Dollar General store. Mrs. Lancaster, Richard, Miss Betty and I were taking one of our usual trips to mingle, so I thought. Little did I know that this would be the last time that I would see the Lancaster family and, that when we stepped foot out of the Lancaster house twenty minutes earlier, it would be my grand exit.

I surveyed all of the toys I could take in. I bounced the bouncing balls, handled the shiny Frisbees, slung the Slinkies, and imagined what I could do with that big box of Legos. I picked up a super-sized red bat and white ball. It must have struck up a memory in my mind because immediately I came out of toy-land mode and scanned the aisle for Mrs. Lancaster and Richard. I did not see them. Miss Betty was there still, so I kept playing. I had gotten to know her over the other times we had gone out together to mingle, and she had been very nice to me. As I gazed at the bat and ball Miss Betty crouched down beside me to meet me at eye level. She smelled very sweet and she had an illuminating smile. She held up her index finger as if to make a pact with me. She gently took my hand and pressed my index finger to hers, kind of like when you become blood sisters with your best friend in kindergarten. While we pressed our fingers together, I fixed my eyes back on the red bat and ball and wondered again where Mrs. Lancaster and Richard were. Miss Betty embraced me as we began to walk around the store and I continued to search the aisles. Still, I didn't see them. We went through the check out lane and out the door. Still didn't find them. We got into Miss Betty's mint green Monte Carlo. I sat in the back seat with my red bat and ball in hand. We drove away from the Dollar General store, away from the neighborhood and away from the city of Shelbyville, KY. When I realized that we had come upon unfamiliar road, being the highway headed west to Louisville, KY, I began to cry aloud. "I want mama! I want Richard!" Crocodile tears dropped from my face, rolled off of the red bat and fell into my lap. A strange feeling came over me; the feeling that a plant would feel being repotted or pruned; being stripped of parts of itself that had become familiar. Something kept telling me that I wouldn't see Mrs. Lancaster, Richard or any of the other ones I had lived with for the rest of my life. I was being repotted and watered to bring forth future growth. The process of pruning doesn't feel good at first entering it. Being a young seedling, I had no choice but to go with the flow. I couldn't speak the words of the feelings I felt, so I simply had to experience the unknown! What an adventure! (*I wonder if we played baseball?!*)

Alone to Surrounded

*At first I felt all alone. Abandoned! No one to hold me, no
one who could know me.
I called out into the emptiness inside of myself, no one
heard my cry!
I asked God what was going on and He said that He had
everything under control
So...
I had to roll with the punches. Go with the flow.
Little did I know that the river would begin to flow as
quickly as I drifted on its waves.
It took me many places and showed me many graces; New
faces.
People heard me calling from inside of myself, somehow,
and they were there to listen
When I cried out "Here I am!" They wanted to find me, like
an exciting game of hide and seek.
And they found me, shivering inside and anticipating the
next experience to come!
Surrounded...*

We parked outside of a blue and tan apartment building after about two hours of driving, and stopping at McDonald's for a happy meal. "We're here!" Miss Betty said with excitement as she turned to smile at me. I sat in the back seat, seat-belted in, with red bat and ball in one hand and happy meal in the other. My face was sticky from tears, but I attempted to crack a smile. I felt like I was in good hands, but I just couldn't understand why Mrs. Lancaster and Richard were nowhere to be found. I needed a kiss on my forehead right about now.

Miss Betty lifted the driver's seat forward and unlatched my seat belt. She took the bat and ball and sat it on the seat beside me. She ever-so-gently picked me up and carried me to the second floor of the apartment building. When we walked in, I felt a sense of peace and tranquility. A new and unfamiliar place sat before me, and I just kept drifting.

We sat at the kitchen table beyond the living room, and ate our lunch. Afterwards, I was introduced to my very own room. A cozy little room it was. There was a twin bed draped with a brightly colored floral bed spread and pillow sham to match. A small pearl colored night stand stood beside the bed. On top of it sat a dainty little purple lamp. A dresser to match stood across the room. I looked at myself in the mirror attached to it and saw comfort in my face, but I still wanted to go inside of myself and spin and spin and spin until I didn't feel anything unfamiliar. (As a matter of fact, I think I did go there for a few seconds.)

"Here are some toys! This is your doll. Here is a bouncing ball we'll take to the park with your red bat and ball. A jump rope. And this is Simon." (*You know the game that you follow and try to repeat the light sequences.*) Miss Betty showed me the toys she had waiting. I liked them all, but my eyes kept getting fixed on this fancy box that sat in the middle of the pearl colored dresser. Miss Betty picked it up and opened it to reveal a twirling ballerina on the inside of it. It played the most enchanting tune as the beautiful little ballerina twirled. I was mesmerized! She looked like how I felt on the inside when I withdrew to my secret place to find familiarity. The music box was my favorite because of the ballerina. *(I wonder if we played baseball...)*

I adjusted well to my new surroundings. Miss Betty sang to me each morning she woke me up. "Good morning to you! Good morning to you! I thank God for keeping you safe through the night! Thanking God is the way to start every day! GOOD MORNING ANGEL!" Her sweet voice penetrated my sleeping soul, and every morning I awoke from my dreams… many dreams that would soon stage the experiences of my life. Somehow, I cajoled myself into reality from dreamland… and thoughts of the ballerina bounced around in my mind. I watched her allegro, maintain aplomb. And arabesque. And plie'… and then I stretched, and yawned, and sat up to see the box which enclosed the dancing ballerina! Each time, before I arose from the bed, I went inside of myself and spun and spun… until I didn't feel anything unfamiliar…

…Early in the morning new mercies I see! (*I wondered if we played baseball…*)

One morning I arose from the bed, and went out to see Mama moving around the apartment a little more rapidly than I'd ever seen her (in the morning that is…). And as I arose, I experienced allegro, maintained aplomb. And posed in arabesque… And plie'… then stood still with my feet planted firmly on the ground. The ground, meaning the path set before me. That morning I began to walk it out!

Now walk it out… now walk it out! For now we know, that all things work together for the good of them who love the LORD! We walk by faith, and not by sight…

That day, me and my mama, Miss Betty Jean Wilson (Washington was her maiden name) went to Lexington. I remember, on the way down the highway, near a familiar place, mama pulled over to the shoulder and took a nap. I wondered, at first, why she did this. But there was something familiar about this highway, so I just marinated in the feeling of not spinning on the inside. As my mama napped I gazed at her being. I believe this was the first time I had really looked at her. She was a very attractive woman. She had a dark brown complexion; like the color of chocolate icing on a homemade birthday cake. She wore her hair in a medium sized afro style, which framed her thin face perfectly. Her thin frame sat comfortably in the driver's seat as she napped, and I gazed upon her being. I kept staring at her for the approximate thirty minutes we remained on the shoulder of I-64 east. When she raised her head up from her short slumber, I quickly turned to look out the window, not wanting to startle her with my strong stare. We continued on our road trip which would take us to another city in Kentucky called Lexington. This is where my new family tree began to stretch far and wide.

"This is Nanny's house. This is where my mommy lives." mama informed me.
At that moment I remembered the night I had awoken in a tizzy of tears and hysteria. I cried out for my mama! "I want mama! I want mama!" I couldn't move from my bed, and it felt like an ocean pushing through floodgates inside

of me. Miss Betty had come into my room and turned on the little purple lamp. She wrapped her arms around me and said "I'm your mommy now." She held me and assured me that everything was going to be fine. She told me that God wanted her to be my mommy now and that she also wanted me to be her daughter. I remembered her rocking me, sticky face and all, until I drifted off to sleep.

I looked around at the buildings that surrounded me. They didn't look like our apartment. It was a different neighborhood too. The buildings were built of brownish-red bricks. They stretched long across a block or so a piece. About five or six doors with small porches filed down the buildings. More and more of the same kinds of buildings wound around the circular blocks for as far as I could see.

"Well here they are. Hi there!" called out an enthusiastic voice. "Yes indeedy! Yes indeedy!" An attractive older woman stood in one of the doors with a look of amazement on her face. She was a chocolate icing complexion too. She wore short curly hairstyle and glasses sat gently on the ridge of her nose. She wore a sky blue house coat with silver buttons and a pair of black house slippers.

"There is nanny! She is your grandmother." Mama told me as she extended her hand out for me to grab it.

With my red bat and ball in hand I stepped out of the Monte Carlo and walked, with my mama, into Nanny's house.

"Oh! Look at her! She's so beautiful!"

"Hi! Angel! You are so cute!"

"Guess we better go pull out the grill 'round the corner!"

An array of voices, faces, caresses and love taps surrounded me from every side! So many new faces appeared so quickly, I didn't know how to react. I'm sure that I retreated expeditiously into my secret closet on the inside to catch a breath or two.

The commotion continued for what seemed like another of my own lifetimes.

"I'm glad yall finaly got here! We been waitin' and waitin' on yall!"

"Here's my new little cousin!"

"Betty, what you doin' with that white baby!" jokingly shouted a boisterous male voice, which I would learn later, belonged to one of my infamous Washington uncles.

Simultaneously, a slew of voices responded "Oh hush yo' mouth Fred! You so silly!" Everyone just laughed and fellowshipped as if it were some type of holiday.

As everyone settled down around the small living room of my new grandmother's project apartment I clung to my mama. Throughout the evening many other family members and friends of the family and neighbors came in and out. They brought smiles, gifts, food, and encouraging words and excitement. With so much excitement surrounding me, and me not being able to escape it, I began to feel overwhelmed and the floodgates began to quiver inside of me. I tried my best to hold onto the flash flood, but inevitably it came crashing through and tears flooded the room.

As time went on, our visits to Lexington became more frequent and my new family tree grew greater and greater. I became familiar with our family. I had a favorite cousin who was less than a month younger than I. We became very close and spent a lot of time together. I grew to expect the systematic trips to Lexington and enjoyed the parties we had on almost every holiday. Memorial Day, Fourth of July, Labor Day, Thanksgiving, Christmas, and back around to Easter. There was always food, fun and family to indulge in. Not so much, now, did I visit the secret closet on the inside; but I was always glad that place was available for a quick vacation if need be. I went from feeling alone to being surrounded by love and kindness. I guess this would become known as the point in my life where I experienced the Lord opening up a window and pouring out a blessing that I didn't have room to receive!

A few years passed by and me and mama were moving from our second two bedroom apartment into a two bedroom house. From the time mama had adopted me up to now, it had been just the two of us living in our home. Now we moved in with mama's cousins. There were three adults and three children living in this house that would soon become mine and mama's house (amongst others).

I sat on the second pew from the front of our church and watched my mama get married. At six years old, I didn't realize that I had so many emotions inside; especially ones that I could not even explain in my little mind. I anticipated what this new arena of life would bring, and so, as much as I wanted to go, I took a rain check on the trip to my secret place, and sat on that pew in a daze; I just wafted on the hills of the emotional rollercoaster I found myself on. As God had spoken to my heart some six years before, there were my mama and my daddy, right before my very eyes. The house, where Mama and I lived, was now our home. (*I wonder if we played baseball.*)

One summer day, I ran to grab my red bat and ball before leaving with Mr. Stretch (my new daddy). As I ran through the kitchen toward the back door, mama stopped me in my tracks with an immense embrace. She held me close for a few seconds and then kissed me on the cheek. "You can call Mr. Stretch 'Daddy' if you want." She looked deep into my eyes and released me to finish my pursuit out the back door. I ran to the baby blue Volkswagen bug and jumped into the passenger's side seat. Daddy and I went to the park and we played baseball with my red bat and ball!!! So that's what the red bat and ball were for!

Angel Marie Renee' Mayes

Chapter 3
Geometric Growth

"He makes me lie down in green pastures, He leads me beside the still waters."
Psalm 23:2 NKJV

Mama and Daddy sat in the living room watching *"Dallas"* or something of the like while I straightened my shoes in a neat row up against the wall; it was the last thing I had to do before my room-cleaning excursion was complete. As I nestled my white pro-wings closely together and against the wall, I felt a presence behind me. I slowly turned around to find two brown-sugar-skinned little girls standing there staring at me as if to say *'They told us to come in here…'*. I was astonished and bewildered at once, almost going inside of myself, but not. I finished organizing my row of shoes and shifted from kneeling to sitting on the floor. My original intention had been to join Mama and Daddy on the couch, but visitors intercepted that thought. As I sat there I looked upon the two and quickly looked away, not knowing how to react or respond to their stares. They looked to be sisters, one shorter than the other and about two years gap between their ages. I thought to myself, I am six… so the slightly taller one, must be about four or five and the other, tiny one, must be only two or so.

Breaking the muteness and stillness in the room, and feeling like an unexpected belch had just protruded from my lips, I spoke. "Hi...".

"What's your name?" the youngest one of the two, to my surprise, asked.

"Angel." I responded as, again, I looked away. My mind tumbled all over the place. *Who are they? What are they doing here? Does my mama know them? Why didn't she tell me we were expecting company?*

Things went kind of hazy somewhere in that stream of thoughts. I probably went on a short sabbatical! The next thing I know we were all sitting in the living room with Mama and Daddy.

There was an immediate halt to my intermittent vacationing when I heard,

"Daddy? Who is she?"

"*Daddy?*" I thought. "*Is there someone else here?*"

I looked toward the couch, across from the love seat where me and Mama sat, and confirmed that one of the little girls who, moments before, stood in my room, had asked the question. Both of them looked intently upon daddy's face awaiting an answer.

I felt mama's arm around my shoulders as she rubbed my arm as if to comfort me.

"Her name is Angel. She is my daughter too."
Daddy informed the two inquisitive expressions. The two
girls looked at one another with wide eyes and eyebrows
raised. I just looked... somewhere in outer (or inner) space.

"Angel, this is Gabrielle and this is Dana. These are
my daughters." Daddy, (Mr. Stretch, I saw at that particular
point) nodded toward each one as he introduced them.
Mama was still rubbing my arm.

"Hi." was the only thing I could muster up to say.

"Hi." repetitiveness resounded.

Gabrielle, was the older of the two, only about eight
months younger than I, was kind of shy and laid back.
Dana, the tiny, talkative one, was three years old. Later I
would learn that she was really older beyond her literal
years.

Our encounters became more frequent, very
frequent, and soon systematic. At first my two sisters
would come to visit us on the weekends. Then they started
to stay for 'longer weekends'. Eventually we all shared a
household; one big happy blended family. That statement
can be taken figuratively and literally. We were not the
traditional, societal, old fashioned family; meaning that we
were not all blood related. And we were truly a blended
family; if you put Mama and Daddy's chocolate icing

complexions with Gabrielle's and Dana's brown sugar complexions and then added my butter cream complexion, you would probably get a great big batch of cupcakes! I do have to say that we made for a delectable mixture; even with every bitter sweet experience we concocted!

"They are simply beautiful! Are they all your daughters?" comments and questions were constant reflectors of our non-traditional representation. Everywhere we went, I felt anyway, that we, or at least I was a spectacle. Although people showered us with compliments, I, somehow, always felt a sense of insecurity.   "All three of them are simply beautiful! Look at them…" people would say. "Now she's (meaning me, 'butter cream') your daughter too?"

After so many times I became used to the "questioning" and sort of melted into the camaraderie.

My sisters and I did grow to attract a lot of attention. We all were beautiful little girls illuminating grace and poise. We all had extraordinary personalities, each our own, and we loved to enjoy family and friends' fellowship. Now, as most people know, there are two sides to every story, so it must be admitted that we each had our own flaws and shortcomings as all human beings do.

Chapter 4
I Meant To Do That

As time passed by and my family ties began to loop like bunny-ear-tied shoe strings, I began to realize that this life thing is continuous and ever changing. I had endured the rustic years of middle school where I was teased and taunted almost every day. There were the dusty kneed, ashy knuckle beady headed boys on the bus who constantly touched my silky hair, which was usually pulled back into a pony tail so I would not feel so disheveled after the long bus ride home. Then there were girls who had short brittle hair which they gelled back with Pre-Con gel (the brown gel) to make it look silky and straight. Most of the time their clothes were too tight and had stains that were either permanent or evidence of their unwashed attire. I didn't understand why they didn't like me and treated me so badly. They would call me names like half breed and yellow bitch; they would talk about my shoes and clothes which I knew were clean and ironed; I liked my style. I had a neat back pack, with the smooth and soft No. 2 pencils that wrote real smooth; I had the neat red, black and blue erasable pens, and a Trapper Keeper with purple, orange and white designs on it; I thought I was a pretty cool kid and a good friend. I didn't tease them about their beady or brittle hair, or their funny looking clothes, or the fact that they didn't have back packs, Trapper Keepers or pencils. I tried to befriend some of the girls on my bus, but they didn't know how to be my friend beyond the jealousy that entrapped their minds. Needless to say, I did not have many friends in my urban neighborhood in West Louisville, Kentucky. However, I did have a few friends at school; we compared our No. 2 pencils, complimented one another's back packs and purses, encouraged one another to score high on tests and quizzes, did our homework together, and planned out our outfits and hairstyles together. Some of the boys at my school were even cool. They would play pencil break, but never with the smooth and soft No. 2 pencils. One of my good friends in middle school was named T.J.

One scorching hot summer day, T.J and I started out for our summer day camp. We were so excited because first, we were traveling alone on public transportation and second, because we were going to high school this year at most hype high school in the city, Central High.

"Yeah!! We gon' be some "yellow jackets" in exactly three weeks and three days!" T.J. exclaimed to me as she pulled her planner out of her handbag. We had started preparing for our high-school-girl-look early on, so we had to carry our purses, with all of our important, personal and private stuff neatly organized inside.

"I know! I can't wait 'til the first day of school so I can see all of the finest dudes in the 'Ville at our school!!!" I replied with a high five waiting for T.J. We slapped hands and laughed out loud. (LOL!)

"Oh! Here's our stop! You got your swim suit?" T.J. interjected as she replaced her planner into her Liz Claiborne handbag.

"You know it! I can't wait to hit the pool!" I bellowed as I hustled to the front of the bus to exit.

We, two middle school friends, sauntered down the road headed to our summer camp. As we walked we were silent. I breathed in the humid aroma of honey suckles and dandelions. The sun shone down ushering in the glimmer of excitement that came with the beginning of the summer season. A light breeze brushed across my rosy cheeks and caressed my scalp as it ran through my hair which hung down my back free from worry of the disheveling bus ride from middle school. I thought of how I was going to be able to handle high school? I mean, I had a boyfriend in eighth grade, and we had kissed and hunched a couple of times (although I did not mean to), but how was I going to keep up with the pace of the upper classmen who were already there and knew the ropes? I was going to have to learn them and quickly, or else I would be so lost. I thought to myself 'When I get home I'm gonna' do some serious brainstorming on this high school thing.'

T.J. and I signed in with our counselor and headed straight for the pool. We normally spent the summer days swimming, coming out of the pool to eat lunch, sit under the gazebo, for about an hour, rapping with some other youngsters until our food digested and returning to the pool to finish off the day.

T.J. had a caramel complexion, a thin frame and long flowing dark brown hair. She wore it in a low pony tail pulled to the side, where her hair hung over either of her shoulders. She was a very attractive young 'high-schooler", but her personality portrayed Plain Jane.

I felt like a middle-schooler still because most of my middle school friends had been traveling to places alone, besides from school to home, from during the sixth grade school year on up to this summer break before high school. I did not have that leniency from my neck of the woods. So needless to say, I was still kind of wet behind the ears, or "as green as a blade of grass" as some may call it, when it came to canvassing from 'hood to 'hood [neighborhood that is]. By now the sunrays of the summer and the swimming party we'd attended every day for the past three and a half weeks had caused my fair skin tone to a deep tan. My fine textured hair hung down my back, about an inch past the middle of my back, and by now, my chubby body had stretched out only to land the curves and lumps proportionately in all the right places. I did not mean to be so naïve to this reality, but I was! So many boys, well, they looked like boys who had a lot of muscles and facial hair, flapped around us like flounder out of the ocean. We were amazed at the cohort change. We knew the boys we hung with when we rapped and how they joked and wrestled around with us. We were all just cool. But these flounder found us, T.J. and myself, in unknown territory.

We left the pool early that day. Maybe it was the white and black polka dot swim suit I wore. Or maybe it was the green and yellow swirled swim suit with the strap around the neck that T.J. wore. But the two of us, even after putting our two heads together, could not understand why we were hounded by some flounders that day. For the rest of the day we just kicked around the park. I was still thinking about high school. Were those the kinds of boys we had to look forward to?!!

"Hey sexy!" a mature male voice called out as T.J. and I sat conversing on a stoop across from the basketball court. We kept talking.

"Slim! You in the black and white." Again the voice called out.

I looked down at my attire, still the white and black suit only now covered up with my black shorts and my towel hanging around my neck. I looked up to see a virile Dove dark chocolate pair of sexy legs standing in some Nike slide-on sandals. I did not mean to get so caught up that I continue the journey towards the mouth that the voice proceeded from. I meant to keep on talking about my yet-to-come first day of high school. But my lips were still... like peanut butter... and my mouth hung open like a field waiting for harvest. My eyes caressed the air which stood as still as my lips and I blinked as if to pinch myself. I did not mean to fall into the fantasy land that I fell into when I gazed upon this fine specimen who smiled from the mouth which called out seconds earlier. His abs were cut into a six pack of Tahitian treat. His biceps rolled like Tootsies. He stood up straighter and surer than if I had raised both hands! This was a fine looking young man. Like the ones I had seen but had never spoken to or heard speak. I did not mean to receive the kiss he planted on my lips before I left the park that day. But I did and I was mesmerized.... From that point on I was taken to another realm of womanhood. Falling in love. I did not mean to sneak through the bushes to go to his house with him. When we got there I meant to ask him where his mother was, because I was so used to the rule *"no boys in the house when I'm not home"* from my neck of the woods. I meant to leave when he told me she was at work, but I did not. I did not mean to lustfully stare at his naked body when he came out of the bathroom and untied his robe to reveal the whole body and nothing less than the whole body. But I did stare. When he started to try to take my clothes off to join him at his birthday party, I denied him that privilege and I went back to the park, hoping that none of the counselors would see me sneaking back through the bushes. I meant to do that. But I did not mean to continue running into him at the park each day until I wanted to be alone with him. I didn't mean to feel like I wanted to take risks to be with him. But I did take risks to be with him in many different ways. I didn't mean to fall in love or lust at such a young age, but I did. One thing I did mean to do was to live. I meant to do that. And this was one extravagant life experience at one week before my fourteenth birthday. I let myself fall in love, I let myself be loved and lusted after. I liked it at the time and I grew to REALLY like it. Throughout my high school years I let myself live and learn. And I meant to do that!

Angel Marie Renee' Mayes

Chapter 5
Entering In

I strolled down Sutcliffe Avenue sporting my stonewashed jeans with the zippers at the ankles, a red polo shirt and my brand new classic K-Swiss. The excitement of the first day of school overwhelmed my entire being. Not to mention the fact that the young man I had encountered at summer camp was waiting around the corner in his LTD. I could hear the sound of Jodeci's "Stay" coming from his fifteen inch speakers. All the more reason for me to wrestle with the butterflies in my stomach!

When I turned the corner off of the street I lived on I laid eyes on the rumbling, navy blue LTD which was parked beside the bakery on the corner of 36th and Broadway. There he was, this handsome specimen…

"Hey! Hey!" He grinned at me as he opened the passenger's side door. My guilty conscience banged upon my will and said, "DO NOT ENTER!" I, being the stubborn teenager that I was, did not listen to reason and entered at my own will. Shon, the driver, was so handsome pushin' that big blue bucket. He made it look and feel like a luxurious Lincoln. I received front door service from my newfound 'slim' almost every day; he drove me to Central

High from the bakery.

I didn't know that I was about to go into a candy store. I mean, eye candy everywhere!!!

"Whuz up shorty!"

"Dayum!!! Look at that freshman! Slim in the red!"

"Red!"

Voices sang from every which way. They bombarded me until my cheeks hurt from smiling.

My fourth period class was creative writing, and what creativeness our class explored! Central was a predominantly black school with a few white students scattered throughout, but my creative writing class was about half and half.

Mr. Jarboe, our teacher, called out the names on the roll after directing us to give our preferred name. "Jermaine Cook?" Jermaine, who we soon began calling 'Germy' due to his slovenly sloppy appearance on a daily basis, raised his hand to acknowledge his presence. The roll call continued and Vonnie, who became the class clown, answered "Ffflllooowwww--er!" (as if to imitate the skunk on Bambi). The entire class cracked up simultaneously and was scolded by a scowling Mr. Jarboe. From that day on, though, Mr. Jarboe referred to Vonnie as "Flower"! Not one time of him calling on her was there not a chuckle at the least.

About five of us cliqued up from creative writing class, and, along with some other friends from our middle schools, we became the well-known freshman crew of Central High School. Everybody in the school knew us, and nobody messed with any of us, because our crew consisted of females from beat-you-with-a-bat broads to pretty-prissy-and-primping princesses! Either they loved us or hated us. Either way, we were still the coolest of the coolest at Central High!

Angel Marie Renee' Mayes

Chapter 6
Stage 1

"Yall know that tonight's the night! After the game we are gonna go to the dance, then we're gonna meet up at Indy's to finalize our scheme moves. We gonna KICK IT tonight!"

This is the typical conversation in the letters passed between the 'Git Fresh Crew' at Central High School in fourth period creative writing class, Friday. Vonnie was the crew leader, or so she thought. Everyone else just let her believe it so that we could just get our weekends poppin'. Rikki was the spoiled one in the crew. All she had to do was just whine a little bit about everything and anything and we would all just compromise (or not) to get our weekends poppin'. Miss prissy Rikki, cute as she could be, would hear everyone agree with what she wanted and she'd just go with the flow. Then there was Tasha. Comic View! Always makin' a joke to make peace or letting go of her peace to joke on somebody. I'll never forget, ninth grade biology class, she would always smooth out the stress by joking on herself. For example, you know about "the twins"? Well, hers were her best friends in Biology class, 'cause Miss Stephenson was a doozy, strict as could be. Tasha would somehow get everyone's attention, except

Miss Stephenson's, and show us how her "twins" (her two bodacious breasts) acted as her pillow in boring Bio. Hilarious! Nelly. She had the rap for the crew. Always comin' up with the reason and the reasoning behind the schemes. She lived with her grandmother, in the hood by the way, who thought she and all of her friends were just angels. For God's sake! She had the rap. Okay. Okay! Yeah, I was in the "Git Fresh Crew". I was just a cool mama, with schemes of my own. Yeah, I was with the schemin' plan, but I always had my own tricks up my sleeve. Some REAL tricks! I was goin' to the game, the dance and Indy's, but I always had the meet-up place on lock for Saturday afternoon. The Galleria, fo' sho'. Again, I had tricks up my sleeve. Of course, my road dog, Toy, was the real leader of the crew. Always holdin' it down and keepin' it real. Just smilin' and struttin' in all the places; lettin' 'em know, in their faces, whenever it was a let-it-be-known moment. In yo' face! AND what?!! You be the blunden! ("blunden" is a slang word that was used which meant "fool"). Yonnie was laid back. Just laid back. She had tricks up her sleeve too. She and I ran track together. Know that! She moved to Atlanta in the middle of the debut of the "Crew".

So, anyway, back to the beginning where the story

began. Toy, who was not in any of our classes at Central, had given the "letter" to Vonnie at lunch when they got MIA (missing in action). Nobody in the cru worried, 'cause we all knew that they were out on one of their missions, hookin' up the weekend. WE were too busy in the senior lunchroom snorting and spitting peaches just to let it be known that the crew was in the school house! Yeah, yeah, yeah, yeah! YEAH! YEAH! Aww yeah! (Remember the Oaktown 357 song! LOL!)

After lunch we all met up in the balcony between the ninth grade side and the upper classmen's side. Always in a huddle, nobody ever knew but always wondered what we were up to and how we were just so cool. Some of the upper classmen guys would always, never fail to gain our attention, so they thought… but they were really interrupting our meeting. Nevertheless, Rikki, Yonnie and I always occupied the curiosity of the boys while the rest of the crew continued with the exchange of important information. This particular Friday was an extraordinary one.

In our fifth period classes most of us were separated. Nelly and I were in the same class, Spanish. She laid a note on my desk which was right in front of the classroom door as she made her way completely across the room in front of the chalk board. We had sat next to each other for the first few weeks of school but were separated due to our many English conversations which consisted of everything but school and much less Spanish. I settled into my desk, pulled out my materials for class and anxiously opened the folded note. It read *"This is the deal: Friday the game plan sticks. Changes occur after and in between that and Indy's. Toy and Vonnie done came up on some type of hustle where we are all gonna be financially straight for the rest of football season! You know we gotta get those dresses we saw in Bacon's for homecoming night. Everyone else, except Rikki and Yonnie are down, but they will be too, soon as they read the news. We'll talk about the details tonight over the phone."*

"María!?" called Señorita Sachez, "Can you explain to the class the meaning of this story?"

I had so much running through my mind from what I was going to wear tonight, to how I was going to rearrange my schedule to fit the crew's new plan, to what in the world this hustle could possibly be. "No Señorita. No se." Needless to say I was reprimanded and given a weekend assignment to complete and present to the class on Monday. Great, now I had another issue to add to the many already swarming through my mind. I thought about these and tried to figure out how I was going to fit all of this into my weekend for the rest of the day until the bell rang. I didn't have very long to solve this dilemma. When I arrived home would be the time for me to fill my parents in on the details of where, when and with whom I was going for the next, at least, twenty-four hours.

On the TARC stop and during the ride home we all had time to confer and get things in order and be on the same page with each other and our families. We would go home, gather our clothes and meet up at Rikki's house at seven o'clock sharp. Then the masquerade would begin. "What about this hustle that's causing all of the changes in the regular plans for Friday nights?" Yonnie inquired as Vonnie and Toy exited the TARC. "Oh, we'll fill you in at Rikki's; seven o'clock sharp!" they both responded and high- fived each other with a chuckle. "Okay, as long as it does not mess up my plans with Rey-Rey. Hmmm. I got something for him tonight!"

"Yeah, me too!" I agreed. "Not Rey-Rey," I assured Yonnie "but you know who!" We laughed and high-fived in agreement.

As we departed to prepare for the night, I walked slowly trying to put everything into perspective. By the time I arrived home I had the perfect plan to complete every one of my tasks at hand. Before I knew it the time had ticked all the way to six thirty. It was about time to throw my satchel over my shoulder and strike out to Rikki's. I did not want to miss a beat of the meeting as to keep my plans flowing smoothly. I threw my Spanish notebook in my satchel along with some other choice items, "Clothes, shoes, lip gloss, shoe strings..." I checked off items in my head as I called them aloud and then the phone rang, it was Shon... butterflies fluttered.... Humming birds sang.... Waterfalls gushed down mountainsides... rainbows thrust like prisms.... Sun rays gently caressed my face...

Chapter 7
Stage 2

"Okay, mama... I'm 'bout to go over Rikki's. I love you." I informed my mother as I kissed her on the cheek.

"Alright. I love you too." she confirmed. "Be very careful, and call me when you get there!"

Mama always reminded me to check in anytime I was leaving one place to go to another.

I agreed and anxiously trotted down the steps of the front porch with my satchel slung over my shoulder.

The phone call I had participated in beforehand had me on edge. Shon had asked me to meet him at our spot when I told him I was leaving for Rikki's, but I wasn't ready to hook up with him just yet. I had to make the meeting and it was for the "Git Fresh Crew" members only to ensure our plans stayed with only us and didn't seep out. There were too many paths that had to be covered and we didn't need any detours! It was a must that everyone's ground was covered correctly. No one could afford to get caught out of place or we would all be screwed for the rest of our freshman year!

"I'll just tell him that Daddy's leaving with his friends in a minute... so I would meet him somewhere at around 8:30" I thought. But then I changed my mind, not knowing the outcome of the meeting and the crew's timing. Although every one of us would go our separate ways at some point that evening after the dance, I didn't know when or where, so…

No sooner than I had that thought, I heard the sounds of Jodeci's- "So You're Havin' My Baby"- coming from the infamous fifteens mounted in the LTD. My heart began to pound in my chest even harder than the booming speakers because of the smile that spread across Shon's face, and my thoughts were getting confused. Too much was going on and I was doing too much, but nevertheless, I continued on my journey.

"Hi sexy! Come on! Get in!" Shon motioned with his hand for me to join him in the front seat.

"I'm goin' over Rikki's first." I tried to convince him, with my perplexed expression, to go ahead and leave; my cajoling did not sway him. He got out and opened the passenger side door and kissed me on the cheek.

There lay a single red rose, on the dash board in front of me, bouncing to the beat of the music which sounded sooooo good to me.

"Do you know where Rikki lives?" I shouted over the music.

Shon was not headed towards the direction I was headed in, so I took it upon myself to turn the music down and pushed the wrong button switching the song from Jodeci to Scarface's "Goin' Down". As I listened to the words of the song and saw Shon boppin' to the beat, I thought, 'I guess we can ride for a minute and then pull up to Rikki's playing this, 'cause it is goin' down tonight!' Scarface sang *"Please excuse my attitude/ sorry if I'm being rude/ but I got something' to say to you/ hoping you won't lose your cool/ I wanna sneak you out to play with me/ you can spend the day with me/ and we can ride and see the sights/ it's goin' down tonight!"*

We pulled up into a driveway in front of a gray and white house in a neighborhood I knew nothing about, but suddenly I remembered that this driveway was the one I walked up to and away from the day I had snuck from the summer camp to see Shon. "I gotta get to Rikki's." I informed Shon again peering at my watch which read 7:08pm. Upon seeing that, my heart began to pound even faster in my chest. I was supposed to be calling mama by now. I could have walked to Rikki's twice already!!

"Okay! Im'ma take you; I just gotta run in and get something." Shon puckered his lips and blew me a kiss as he exited the vehicle. The music continued to play mixing with the sound systems of other vehicles which were parked up and down the street in various driveways.

I began to relax when Shon returned, knowing that it should only take about five minutes to get to Rikki's house.

"I'll call you later… when we're leaving for the game!" I winked at this handsome specimen as I threw my satchel over my shoulder.

"I'll pick yall up and take yall to the game. Call my cell." He called out the phone number as he pulled a plug out of a black bag and stuck it into the lighter socket below the JVC deck with equalizer. I shut the door and he skeet-skirted down 34th street blasting Scarface.

I rushed into Rikki's house to get the down-low for the evening. Before I set my mind on what this night would consist of, I called my mother and tried to speak in a nonchalant voice.

"Hey mama. I'm here."

"Who is taking you all to the dance? And who is picking you up?" she asked in a calm, detective-style tone.

My mouth stood open as if to will an acceptable answer out of it. I paused, my heart pounded…and then the words tumbled out without me knowing what they would be until I heard them. "I think we're taking the bus."

Mama paused as if she was thinking of another question or waiting for me to say something else. Then she responded "Alright. Be very careful!"

After hanging up the phone, I rested my satchel beside the crew's piles of purses and jackets on the couch and joined the crew in the kitchen where my tall glass of grape Kool-aid awaited me. I gulped the delectable potion down as I anticipated the information to come.

"Okay, we already got the plan 'cause you were taking too long to get here and we need to be leaving here soon." Vonnie nudged my shoulder as she spilled out the plan for the crew.

Monday morning rolled around and, as usual, I met Shon at our normal spot for a ride to school. This daily meeting had become the norm because, if I didn't see him at the spot, I saw him in the hallway near my locker or on the way to class. I don't know how he knew so much about or spent so much time in the hallways at Central High seeing that he was a senior at a high school way across town. It was kind of cool at first, but then it became annoying. I didn't have any space to be with my friends and talk about our weekend adventures because he was always up in the mix, interrupting and asking questions!

I kissed Shon and got out of the car, hoping he

would bump his music and leave. He did. But inevitably there sounded off the sounds of Jodeci from the parking lot during fourth period.

"He's baa--aa-ck!" Vonnie shouted aloud. Although the entire class didn't know who 'he' was, they thought she was being the normal class clown, and responded to her joking with a resounding "Guess who?!" followed by chuckling and cackling.

I didn't find it very funny, so I concentrated on the assignment Mr. Jarboe had given and pretended not to hear even the music rattling the windows of the classroom.

When fourth period ended I headed towards my locker. Here comes Toy from the Git Fresh Crew, the informant, telling me that Shon is downstairs questioning people about who I was dancing with on Friday.

"Giirrrrllll! You betta go get him. You know Rallos and 'em ain't havin' 'et! They talkin' 'bout gettin' him afta school! Go tell him to go back to his school!"

I followed the bell signals for the rest of the day and sure enough the sounds of Jodeci awaited my arrival in the parking lot. When we pulled off the parking lot, I saw my crew on the bus stop. Shon skeet-skirted through the light and we were sliding down Broadway to the beats of Scarface.

Shon pulled into his driveway at approximately 2:41pm (I kept time on the gold nugget watch he'd given me to make sure I was home before Mama). He turned off the music and slid me over towards him clutching me under his arm.

"I don't want you hangin' wit' none of them j-birds at your school. You my baby! They all smoke and drank and I don't want you in none of that! Okay sexy?" he squeezed me tight and motioned me to come in the house.

"I got something for you!" Shon pulled out a white teddy bear with a red ribbon around its neck and a red rose stuck between its paws.

I blushed and smiled. "Thank you…" I responded shyly not knowing how to receive his gestures.

By the time we left his house, my rectum was throbbing and my face was burning from his alleged 'accidental sodomy'. On the ride back to our meeting spot, around the corner from my house, I retreated into that familiar place… that intrinsic escape… the secret closet inside of the big space inside of me, where I felt safe… there were no butterflies or humming birds… just dead flowers and dried up streams. As I shut the door to the LTD, Shon said, "I love you…! See you in the morning!"

I vomited inside of me, forced a smile out of one

side of my scorched face, and waddled down the street racing for the cold seat of the bathtub.

Chapter 8
Switch!!! But Whyyyy?

"He restores my soul; He leads me in the paths of
righteousness for His name's sake."   *Psalm 23:3*
NKJV

Even though my academic grades were good my
freshman year, I would not be returning to Central High for
my sophomore year. I guess all of my scattered schemes,
forced confusion, and frequent tardiness to school and
home, had caught up with me.

Mama informed me that, when I returned from
Lexington from the summer stay with my grandmother,
(not by choice, but required as a punishment), I would be
enrolling at a different high school.

"But why?"- I pled with my mother to no avail.

So for one year I grudgingly walked the halls at
Butler High School. Still, my grades were exceptional, but
my place of retreat had become many, if you know what I
mean. I guess that I felt like I had to redeem myself (or my
thought process about love and relationships) from sodomy.
So I attempted many redemptive tactics. Unknowingly, I
plastered myself into a cylindrical tunnel of turmoil and
confusion. Now, that inner place of peace was like a
warring rave fostering rage and depression. Sure fire…

Psalm 23: The Lord is my Shepherd; I shall not want. He looks after me, and that means I have everything I need- (even in the sure fire). Because He makes me lay down in green pastures and He leads me beside the still waters- (even the cold seat of the bath tub).

After that year of high school...

Our family relocated to a city on the West Coast set in a valley and surrounded by mountains. In Kentucky we were used to humid summers where outside felt like a hot swimming pool. I remember the summer programs I attended and how the small white Styrofoam cups filled with ice water at lunch time became our best friend for the rest of the day as we raced back and forth to the water fountain for refills to relieve us from the laps we swam in the hot pool of humidity outside. Wintertime in Louisville always dumped inches or feet of snow on the streets and rooftops. School would be called off due to the large amounts of snowfall and we would bundle up in bubble coats, toboggans, gloves and boots before we trudged out into the neighborhood for an adventure or a snowball fight. We had moved to a desert valley in northern Nevada which yielded summers as dry as a pair of powdery chapped lips and hotter than the spice of a Carolina reaper pepper! The winters were frigid, but we rarely had white Christmases. The largest amount of snow this valley offered was a dusting at most; peering upward from the valley floor would give sight of snowcapped mountaintops throughout the winter and far into the summer weeks.

Talk about culture shock! We had lived in the urban city life of Louisville, Kentucky for the past eight and a half years. Black faces made up the majority of the conglomerate of 'hoods. You could always find a barbeque with some good old school music setting the atmosphere. "Love Train", "Family Reunion", "For the Love of Money" by the O'Jays were classics for holiday gatherings. Weekends were holidays for the 'hoods we knew. Rolling down the streets were old school Chevy Impalas, Buick '88s, LTDs, short-cut, long-cut, and box-cut Caddies (Cadillacs), and even hoopties were cool for the 'elite'. Low riders, hydraulics, under-cab black lights, mirror-tinted windows and bras for the grills were some of the accessories to go along with the JVC sound systems amongst many others that competed in the streets. The drivers were draped in one to four-inch wide, eighteen to twenty-four-inch long herringbone and rope chains, twenty-four carat gold, diamond-cut rings that stretched across each and every finger, gold nugget and Rolex watches, dope man Nikes, and a choice of Guess?, MCM, Gucci or Louis Vuitton threads. Whomever had the most in their collection of "collectibles" was considered a "big baller" and a "shot caller". And that's not to mention the great melt- down of the gold rush! There had to be at least two gold teeth in your mouth for you to be considered amongst the 'elite' of the ghetto. Now that was for the male side of the fence. On the other side were the females. The requirements were pretty much the same as for the male 'elite' induction except your "collectibles" had to be gentle and dainty in a ghetto-fabulous way, if you know what I mean. LOL! If you were a female and you did not like 2Pac, that was your first strike- and you were out! Clubbin' was a must! You had to be able to get in, even if you were under-age, to all the hypest clubs- or else it was over for your initiation. If you were in the parking lot all the time, then you were just a mark or a buster!

I was aware and understood the requirements the 'hoods had set for one to either get in or fit in, but I was never much interested in all of that. I did like some of the Guess? jeans that a few of my friends wore, and the Louis Vuitton and Liz Claiborne bags they carried, but I never felt like those things could make me or break me. I liked being me. I liked my simple style; clean, neat, matching, and left a little sumpin' sumpin' to the imagination. I did enjoy my times of observation; something about all the competition was just fun. When we were uprooted from this life to move on to another part of our journey, I felt like I would not be able to function without the *"something-'bout-the-'hood-just-makes-you-feel-good"* atmosphere.

God must have known that it was time for me to be restored before I fell into destruction. So in all of His gloriousness and omniscience God made a drastic change in my family's atmosphere. We didn't live in an urban area in Nevada, but a suburban area. Most of our neighbors were Caucasian with a few spicy Hispanics scattered about. We no longer rode a bus to school, but walked around the corner to the neighborhood high school. The smoky smell of the barbeque grills from Louisville's 'hoods were replaced with the sound of water sprinklers to water the parched grass and falling ashes from the brush fires in the mountains. The summer before my junior year of high school I had a literal "Social Studies lesson" I will call "What happens here?"

"He may not come when you want Him, but He's always right on time!" That's what mama would always say. I just didn't want this time, my last two years of high school, to be His "on time"!

"But whhhyyyyyy????!!!" I kept asking… someone, anyone, and everyone!

And someone answered…..Why not?

Chapter 9
Sing Unto The Lord a New Song!

Be still and know that He is God

Two weeks after I graduated from high school, around 4:30am, after the last night of my residence in Sparks, Nevada, after Camp Anytown- Bethel AME Church, Young Peezy, University of Reno frat parties, a 4.0 GPA senior year after appearing before a Judge, keeping my driver's license, Jack 'n the Box, and my acceptance of Jesus Christ as Lord and Savior, I awoke to my mother's still sweet voice awaking me to take up my cross and follow Jesus.

At seventeen years old, I was, entering into my first real valley. Only God… and I knew what was really happening. Taking up ALL of me… and going…
If you paid attention, even a little, in Language Arts class, you will understand the ellipsis or dots after a word, statement, phrase, sentence, feeling… etcetera…
Going on to another place in HIM…
*…As I sit here (**at 33 years old, and write and reminisce**)… and try… I look at the things GOD has provided me…*
And I am still grateful!
…on to the days in which disappointment infused with

anticipation curdled my mind.

First we must get an understanding of the curdling process… to coagulate… to drive… to cause to become somewhat firm… a firm substance covered in a fluid substance… think of it like this; You wake up on a Saturday morning anticipating a bowl of Captain Crunch. You pull the bowl from the cabinet, pour the cereal, go turn on your favorite cartoon, come back into the kitchen, grab your favorite spoon with the red handle, open the refrigerator, get the carton of milk, open it… and … you take a second whiff only to smell a stench! WHAT!!!

Now, once I had relocated from my two year prior, reluctant relocation, there were crestfallen consequences and intercepted endeavors awaiting my ordained arrival. The chapter I had pretended to close, one and a half years prior, came back to dishevel my future. There, in that still place, some obstacles attempted to obliterate the opportunities of my life time. (Meaning to cause me to fall and be destroyed…) What the devil meant for bad…. God Almighty meant it for my good! (That is the 20/20 vision of the present- you know, what hind sight always is.)

What started off the frenzy of my newfound voyage was the backtracking of my footsteps into the path of a familiar acquaintance of the Git Fresh Crew. Shon, "Mr.

Sexy Lover Man" as he called himself by now, waited at the baggage claim with my luggage already in hand. A wide faced grin crawled across his face as he reached to pull me into his torso. He hugged me tight and spun me around like on the movies.

"Oh wow! Is this what we ridin' in?!" I bellowed as if to have just heard an original song of mine being played on the radio for the first time. I looked at the snow white drop top mustang with peanut butter seats and shiny chrome rims whose trunk Shon opened.

"Yeah baby! You know how I got to do it for my Pooh Bear!" he assured me as he shut the trunk.

"You know we gots to ball! You know meeeee-eeee!" Shon opened the passenger side door as he vociferated his "big baller" mentality.

Inside of me there was a familiar feeling far off in a faint place. Something like uneasy, shy, or embarrassed; possibly all of them tangled up in one big snowball effect. I remembered a place I used to visit quite frequently as a child; I vacationed there for a few minutes… at least until I was returned back to reality on 264 West. We were passing by Wyandotte Park where my friends and I used to go swimming. Thoughts reminded me of the pool we passed by being an escape from Shon two years prior, and now here I was riding right by my very hiding place with the intruder at my side! I shook my head as if to remove the memories from my being…

"Wo! Should I be arranging an escape?" My childhood-self tried to shake me to consciousness from the qualms I'd fallen into after remembering past entrapments with "Mr. Sexy Lover Man".

Nonetheless, business went as usual with me and Shon. I ignored my deepest doubts and fears to keep him satisfied. So much remained for me to experience with this young man…. I had not an inkling of an idea- even as closely juxtaposed as the Ohio River is to the Second Street Bridge- what awaited in store for me.

A quick memoir should exemplify the roads I traveled… again…

leaving my friends and the plans we had made to jump to his beckoning call… laying on the waterbed terrified that he would try to sic the dog on me if I did not cooperate with his every wish… arguing about where I had been and whom I had "been with"… being accused of screwing every male who was a human… being followed… threatened…. stalked… afraid… feeling inadequate… crying frequently… doing sexual favors to avoid abusive treatment… standing in front of him holding a car jack over

his shoulder in position to swing it at me... taking out a
restraining order... falling into the trap of mental and
emotional abuse at seventeen years of age...

"Can I get a quick hiatus?" pleaded my childhood self...

There is no easy escape from abuse... some learn to
cope with it, some learn to ignore it, and others learn to live
with it. Of course, being the well-rounded youth I was, I
took the high road and attempted to master all three. In this
school of hard knocks I was enrolling in the second
semester with two required electives. One elective was in
Human Services and the other in Social Services....

Now we're really singing... there will be sad songs
to make you cry... "love" songs often do...

Here I was... still....

Angel Marie Renee' Mayes

Chapter 10
Claustrophobia

The abnormal dread of being in closed in or narrow spaces. Think about every negative, scary, unexpected, exciting, unplanned, and/or embarrassing experience you have ever had. Now think about not overcoming them… now imagine at least two of them always manifesting somewhere or somehow in your life every day, every week, every month, every year! How debilitating it is to have so many demons to haunt you when you try to treat people right, you know… not judging them, loving them unconditionally, looking beyond their faults and seeing their needs. Sometimes we can do this without knowing that we are not doing the same for ourselves. This was the first lesson I was taught in Elective Number One: Social Regulations versus Human Degradation.

On Spalding University's campus, in downtown Louisville, I found myself in a whole new arena. I had clamored through the summer after high school ducking and dodging Shon. My attempts were trumped with the repeated success of the culprit! Now that I had a schedule of classes on top of my job, I thought that there was a chance of escape. Not to mention all of the eye candy on display in the college candy store! This was like a Godiva chocolate superstore contrasting the little corner store at Central High. Wow! I was going to be on numerous of sugar highs!

"Come on yall wanna ride out? We can cruise Broadway and then hit Indy's for a minute. Y'all know the slims is gonna be all ova' the place!" Tresa persuaded our roommates and me.

"Come on y'all! It'll be fun!" agreed Shayla.

Tresa, Shayla and I had gone to high school together before I had moved across the country. We didn't take to kindly to one another then, but now, since we were all roommates, we might as well have let by-gones be by-gones!

We rode down Fourth Street about to turn on Broadway. While we sat at the light at the intersection I heard the flick of a lighter. "Here, yall wanna hit this Black?" Tresa passed a cigar with a white tip on in to the back seat where I sat with our other classmate, Charia. We both looked at the Black and Mild and then at one another... as if to gesture "Geronimo!!!!!!" I grabbed the cigar and hit it.

"Have y'all had Blacks before?" Tresa and Shayla asked as if it were a sin not to have.

"Nope," we responded, searching for the meaning behind the puff of smoke we had just sucked in.

"Well just hit it lightly, don't hit it too hard or you will choke, choke, choke, on that smoke, smoke, smoke!" the two familiar friends chanted-simultaneously as they slapped a high five followed by a snap of the fingers.

Here I was back in the 'hood, and it had changed quite a bit. Possibly I had not been exposed to the reality of the 'hood mentality before I had moved. Tresa bumped the music and laid back in her seat as she bopped her head and the cigar to the beat of the music. The tinted windows on her black Shadow were rolled down enough for us to see out clearly, but right at head level of the front seat riders. As we strolled up and down Broadway numerous times, it didn't become boring as one would think, with us repetitively going back and forth, up and down the same street, the same approximate fifty or so blocks from First Street to Shawnee Park. There were the elite, the ghetto fabulous, the gangstas and the college crews. The cohort didn't change much, only the lifestyles we would all depart to when the strolling and primping was over. As we rode, I observed the packs of young men, who were the gangstas from different sets, draped in all red with bandanas either hiding their faces or being flung around in the air like lassos along with the sign language they were so adamant about displaying. Other groups were draped in blue with pretty much the same behavior. Then there were the big ballers! I mean, the elite I knew about in high school must have grown up because now the herringbones were coupled with ropes and pendants nearing the size of Flava Flav's clock! The cars were no longer Caddy's but Beamers, Benzes, and Lexuses! The old hoopties were no longer hoopties but clean-cut old schools. People pulled over on each side of the street and parked to floss. "To floss" means to show off- see who can out-do who or who catches the most compliments, shows the most money or weed, or pulls the most 'hook-ups', if you know what I mean! Hook-ups happened after hours; people had to creep for these because one man's cousin or brother was probably hookin' up with the other's hook-up from the night before. I was already becoming somewhat claustrophobic and the abnormality was only just beginning!

Surprisingly the frequency of Shon's appearances had lessened. I was glad and leery at the same time. Glad because I could spread my wings and I loved all of the compliments I got when I had room to floss. Leery because I had no idea what Shon had up his sleeve or in the back of his mind. So I definitely had to remain wide-eyed and bushy tailed!

With so much baggage already on my back, upon my return to Kentucky, the extra baggage I acquired in my first semester of college weighed me down and I had forgotten how to retreat to my safe place on the inside. It was cluttered up with Black & Milds, one night stands, Hurricanes (the alcoholic beverage), clubs, blunts, an extremely low G.P.A, promiscuity… and…. only God knows what else.

Needless to say, I had become confused and couldn't focus on my major, much less my future. I didn't even know which way I wanted to go because I had never settled down long enough from the junk that constantly chased me around to know who I was. I was lost and falling…. Maybe that was the meaning of those dreams I had had often as a child; the witch was chasing me and I was falling.

Angel Marie Renee' Mayes

Chapter 11
As the Girl Falls...

"Yea, though I walk through the valley of the shadow of death, I will fear no evil" Psalm 23:4a

With all of the clutter and mess around and inside of me, I had to find a place of retreat, so I became like a hoarder and made one. I just began to step over, ignore and caress all of the mess as if to prompt it to stay down and out of my way. Unaware, I didn't know that I was nurturing the clutter only to cause it to increase. Here we go…
"'round and 'round the mulberry bush, the monkey chased the weasel…"

I had felt that feeling for the last time (or so I thought). You know, that one where you feel like you're going to lose control of yourself. Some people may not know this feeling (falling). You feel like a dirty old rubber band that has lost most of its elasticity; if you snapped, everything would be a disaster. The weasel means to escape from or evade a situation or obligation. The monkey represents a persistent or annoying encumbrance or problem. Now once again, I, the weasel, was being chased by the monkey. Obviously, in hind sight, I wasn't running fast enough or far enough.

It was like a dream of a pleasant man, not bad

looking, with puppy-dog expressions to die for. (That should have been my first red flag! A dog…). He had caught my eye in Central Park… "Central" how ironic! My cousin and I were leaving to go on to the next adventure for the evening when a voice called out "How you doin' love?" The young man grasped the ends of the towel around his neck and gently pulled his bottom lip in. I thought it was sexy, but once again, in hind sight, that is a sign of a rabid dog licking his chops!

"Do I know you?" I replied, subconsciously, hoping my response would send this come-on on its way. We had been at the festival for about two hours and none of the men here were worth even saving their numbers. Besides, by this time I had made a complete evasion from Shon's belligerent oversight, and I was not even entertaining the thought of a relationship… until I found myself on the continued descent again… *NOOOOOOOO!!!!!*

"No! No! NO!" my conscience kept screaming at me. But "Yes! Yes! Yes!" pounded my heart. Especially after the tilt of his head and the kiss he planted on my hand.

"No, sweetheart, you don't know me, but I'd like to get to know you. My name is Sonny. What's yours?" he asked.

"Angel." I shyly replied.

"OH My! God has sent me an angel!" Sonny's bellow seemed to have echoed the entire park.

Once again, clutter would not let me listen to reason, or continue on my journey of single womanhood. I wrote my number down and handed it to him. We left the park…

"Ladies and gentlemen we are on our descent to a crestfallen consequence… please buckle your seatbelts and prepare for extreme turbulence and a very rocky landing."

Extreme turbulence and a rocky landing were mild warnings. This ride became more like a tumble off of a cliff and crashing to the bottom.

A bullet to the temple… a bruise from a bite underneath my right breast, purple and blue, the size of a baseball… knock-down, drag-out battle wounds and scars. Nothingness became everything as I plummeted… chains of weed smoke connected to a plethora of pleasure, or an attempted escape. I was meandering around a maze that seemed to have ended in all dead ends- one way in and no way out. I recall glass vases shattering against the wall behind the force from an angry hand's fling… I felt like a Raggedy-Ann doll who could not stand on my own. Numb and mentally nauseous, I staggered around and about etching out the edges of the cliffs end… fraudulent forces spoke to my shaken character and squashed me, like a Coca-Cola can, into a mentally vegetative state. Zombified inside... zany in my brain...zapped of all sanity...zero summed in a situation, circumstance? Zig-zagged out...down to a zillion times zilch...zonked...so far from Zion... falling... sinking... sin-sick me!

I had lived eighteen years, and now I was dead. Temporary insanity constitutes death of a life. To die is to stop living; to stop functioning; to lose force of activity. I was dying down, ceasing gradually. One never knows when the day or the hour will come... and my dying day came, figuratively... statistically... at a young tender age.

Pimped out, I would learn later, my position was the bottom bitch. Always there to take care of the widower's children, left to bear the burdens of a family dismantled by death. The mother of his children had passed away... and I was "chosen" to fill in the gap. At first I didn't feel the strain of the acute identity crisis, but sooner than later the rubber bands which held my sanity in place would snap, and everything that curdled up and crunched together would spill out with volcanic, vehement, volatile violence... and my brain vomited... and dry-heaved... and fell...

"Wanka-wanka--wanka..." Voices swarmed from

every which way. Charlie Brown's life would have been a great escape, but I couldn't be so fortunate to be a cartoon character at that moment. The demanding voices, or the persuasive jargon that seeped through the 'wanka-wankas' were of the social workers, and the nurses and the doctors tramping tumultuously on the tragedy in which I had so unwillingly secluded my morbid mentality.

"What am I doing here?" I traveled through all of the hoarded, hematic, avenues which had been built in my secret safe place, searching for the peaceful place that was once readily available. After trudging and tripping, slipping and sliding, I found the blood of my lifeline slowly seeping from the tear in my heart… I was slowly, slipping away.

"Come on Marie, it's time for your second meeting. You missed the one this morning. Come on get up. The quicker you get through these meetings the quicker you can get out of here," the nagging voice called.

She had entered the room about four times before I could come back from that place on the inside. I could no longer call it a safe place… after all, I was bleeding internally, and none of these people could ever know that I was dying inside. No x-ray, no CAT scan, no MRI could detect the inner turmoil that was killing me. No meeting, no counselor, no sharing would mend the tear inside of me. I knew that something far greater than any human ability, whether medically or mentally, would have to perform a miracle for me to make it through the trauma. Nonetheless, I had to muster up enough strength to get up and go to the meeting. I didn't want to go into the hallways because I had to face myself. I felt like I was walking in a graveyard where the dead had risen... or were waiting in line at the morgue to be 'cared for'.

I talked to myself, "Seriously, you! Straight 'A' student, graduated with honors! A 4.0 senior year G.P.A! What are you doing here? Why don't you just get it together?"

The lady jumped in my conversation with me. "Because it's a part of your life. God allows a lot of things to happen. We may never understand them, or HIM, but you'll be fine. When you get out of here, you can just keep on going..."

I cried. I smoked a cigarette. I sat still... attempting to see myself going on... I remembered that I was bleeding internally... I cried again. And then I fell into her arms. An older lady she was, about three times my age. I think she was my roommate. She cried with me... and I went on... to the next meeting... and I talked, shared, cried.

"What does life mean to you? What is it to live?

Please share," directed the counselor.

I listened… tears welled up in my eyes. I tried to suck them back up, I couldn't stand to lose any more fluid. Someone, one of the people who had walked the morbid hallways, spoke of life… I looked upon her countenance and she was being freed from bondage as she spoke of life…her bowed down head slowly raised upward, her chin no longer sat on her chest, darkness lifted from beneath her eyes as one tear slid down her pale cheek. Then she cried… and then I shared. "Life is getting better…"

For a few moments more than not, I wasn't falling. I was still not yet out of here and going on… but I wasn't falling right now, so life was getting better.

Angel Marie Renee' Mayes

Chapter 12
A Child is Born...

"I'll show you what limp is… yeah, Imma show you…!" The blood curdling words stung my eardrums. My face and elbows were pressed into the mattress, my shoulders were squeezing my cheek bones, and the scream I attempted to spit out wouldn't or couldn't, escape past my uvula, then I relinquished the sliver of fight I had left in my entire being. The hammering thrusts punctured my once lost innocence and I became the impassioned prisoner to pain, emotionally hurt… My soul was trespassed… beyond the point of no return…

A warm stickiness settled between my thighs as I still lay face down, now alone, in a dungeon. The intruder staggered off to another place. I felt nauseous. I felt the sensation of a profuse cry, but again, along with my scream, my uvula encased it. I knew I was impregnated that day…

Foggy were the days that followed. This young lady was falling somewhere again. I felt so numb and dumb and I thought Mother Nature had even given up on me. I felt sick and tired all the time and I had missed my menstrual cycle although I wasn't really keeping up with time.

7 months later…

As I lay on my left side on the table in the cold room, I waited again for the thump against my womb. There were a couple of kicks from the little life that was growing inside of me.

"Two more months…" I whispered to the fetus as I gently laid my hand on the side of my torso.

"You need to go to the hospital immediately!" my nurse practitioner informed me. As she entered and moved quickly around the room, she jotted information on the padded clipboard, re-checked my blood pressure, and spoke in a very quiet yet alarming voice. "They are expecting you. Go straight to the desk as you enter the emergency room and they will take care of you," instructed the young woman. Baffled and confused I followed her instructions. Later I would find out that my blood pressure was 215/180 and had been slowly elevating over the past few weeks. It would turn out that the substitute for the nurse practitioner had not been correctly taking my blood pressure.

As I walked to my next destination, I thought about the time limit I had in the parking garage at my doctor's office. I wondered why there was such haste in her directing me to the emergency room and I thought about the baby bed I had in lay-a-way. Upon my arrival at the desk I was surrounded by medical people. They pulled a wheelchair up behind me and sat me down as if I suddenly had become and invalid. Somebody took my coat off and wrapped a blood pressure cuff around my right arm. As they wheeled me through the hallways I was prompted to relax… they spoke very softly, almost whispering. The next thing I know, I'm laying on another table conveying through a tunnel-like machine.

"We're just taking pictures of the baby. Just relax," a calm voice spoke.

"Okay…" I responded as I began to become claustrophobic. I tried not to panic at the red and blue lights in the tunnel. I tried to focus on my breathing. I closed my eyes hoping to envision a safe place, somewhere serene. When I felt the change in air pressure I opened my eyes… I was out of the tunnel. *(As Mama always says, THERE IS A LIGHT AT THE END OF THE TUNNEL!)*

"Your baby is doing fine. But we're gonna have to get you in a room immediately!" one of the medical personnel explained to me. "Your blood pressure is extremely high and we need to get that taken care of." My heart pounded hard twice… and then seemed to stop. I followed the directions of the caregivers and soon after found myself in a hospital bed with I.V.s in both arms.

Grogginess overtook me and the last words I heard were "You're gonna have a baby before you leave here!"

Over the next four days I went through a plethora of internal experiences. Twirling around the stage to the song "Black Butterflies"... then fluttering above a field of purple dandelions... I saw humming birds and waterfalls, rainbows and sunshine... I was smiling and smelled the sweet aroma of honeysuckle...

"Hey Angel," one of my sisters reluctantly spoke my name. As my eyelids drew themselves apart, as if honey had become a stream between them, I peered upon the brown sugar faces of my two sisters.

"I'm okay." I quickly responded to the apprehensive expressions upon their countenances. "You can sit down over there. What yall been doin'?" My mental ping- ponged back and forth from honey and brown sugar... Gabby walked out of the room with tears welled up in her eyes. Dana, the brave little sister, told me that they would see me later.

"Okay. Tell Gabrielle I'm okay..." I murmured.

This candy land dream I kept returning to was a wonderful place of retreat, but I never could stay long enough to taste one of the honeysuckles. I remember, as a little girl, my friends and I would find the biggest, prettiest honeysuckles! The sweetness that wisped over my taste buds was a refreshing addition to the warm sunrays that caressed our faces. The next wisp of air I felt was that of the movement from the transporters rolling me down for yet another test, or maybe to surgery this time. I had been prepped for surgery at least twice already… and something must have gone wrong between the preparation and the dissecting sunder of the scalpel. I heard voices and felt a lot of movement around me, but the honey stream between my eyelids had become like a lake, so I could not see anything. I felt comfort from somewhere, so I simply complied.

"Wake up sweety. Wake up…" a small voice prompted me from my place of retreat. "We have to give you anesthesia and then oxygen. You're doing fine, just relax."

The mask seemed to have zeroed in and landed on my face. I felt claustrophobic.

"Just breathe in and out like you normally do," the same voice assured me. I could see a silhouette of a young woman connected to the hand that held onto mine. I just breathed… "Okay they're about to start the surgery in about five minutes. Can you feel that on your right leg? Your left? How about there on your abdomen?" The silhouette asked me a series of questions. Upon each question I shook my head "No".

My body began to jerk back and forth. I could feel the doctors cutting my stomach open. It did not sting or hurt; it just felt like pressure. Some time went by before I was gently nudged from my candy land dream…

"It's a girl!" the silhouette informed me. "We're gonna take good care of her!"

A smile slid across my face as I asked in haste, "Can I see her?"

The silhouette pointed across my face, as I lay prostrate, to the left of me. There in a clear box was my tiny little girl…and I mean tiny! I'd never seen a baby that small… ever! We were separated immediately. She went to the neonatal intensive care unit. I went to recovery. For the next twenty-four hours, or very close to it, I was given reports on mine and my baby's conditions. I still had not seen her face to face. I remember drifting off to some place on the inside for some time… I woke up and there was a body slumped over beside my bed. Shaking myself to reality from twirling and fluttering, I realized that slumped over body belonged to 'my baby's daddy'. He was crying… weeping…

I asked him to wheel me to the nursery to see my baby, but he didn't. I drifted back to search for more honeysuckles.

Majesty

You're Majesty because you're splendid, a royal love in my heart.
A perfect little package, I've loved from the very start.
You bring a special light to my life, one I've never seen before.
And every time I think of you, I love you more and more.
A new turn in life! It feels so good to see...
To have and know and love a special part of me!
God gave you to me, a special gift indeed!
And I assure you that I'll fulfill your every need.
A lovely girl of splendor and magic, so full of joy and light!
Me and you together, the match was perfect and so right!!!

Love, Mommy

I wrote this poem to my darling daughter as I waited for my cousin to come and take me to the hospital to bond with my blessing. Gladness overwhelmed my heart as I remembered the time I made the decision, in obedience to God the Father Almighty, not even eight months prior, not to abort this one. I get JOY when I think about what He's done for me!

Angel Marie Renee' Mayes

Chapter 13
As Life Goes On

"For Thou art with me..." Psalm 23:4b KJV

About fifteen or twenty people showed up along with the two pick-up trucks.

"What's going? What's staying?" The voices of this conglomerate of friends of friends of friends inquired of me. The only finger I had to lift was my right index to point out the items to be moved out of the house. Within one hour, all of our belongings had been moved out of the house we'd lived in with a relative for the past year or so and a year before that year about six months. Nevertheless, Majesty and I were moving into our very own apartment for the second time. It was a quaint little one bedroom apartment, but comfortable and cozy enough for the two of us. This would be an embarking upon, again for me, unfamiliar territory. Oh how I wished that hind sight, before it becomes hind sight, was 20/20. Or to put it in another way, I wish I had known then; what I know now.

Before I could even return with the pizza and sodas, most of my moving crew had departed to venture off on their Friday night excursions. The few who did remain scattered over the parking lot indulged in the pizza and took their Orange Crush to go.

"Okay! See yall later!" my good friend Shay waved good-bye as she tilted her head and smiled sentimentally. (**Fountain of Life**) :)

"A'ight cuz! I'm out! Maybe next weekend you can go out with us! But you know I'll knock a couple back for you tonight!" B Angie B, my cousin, shouted up the steps as she trotted down in front of Shay. B Angie always swept a smile across my face, even in the roughest of tough times.

The two drove off in separate cars to separate destinations as Majesty and I settled into our own new one. As I closed the door I turned around to see boxes upon boxes piled up in the middle of the floor, on the dinette table, on the couch and love seat and on the entertainment stand. I looked at my daughter and back at the massive piles. Tears welled up in my eyes as overwhelm took me almost over the edge. I sobbed into the palms of my hands for some time then plopped onto the arm of the couch crossing my arms. I felt relieved but I also felt somewhat alone. My daughter was there but she was depending on me to keep it together and hold everything down. I gave the apartment another once-over and hung my head to drop some tears from the bucket again. I felt a gentle caress on my face, only to look up to see my daughter's bright light brown eyes twinkling behind her smile as she wiped the tear that slid down my cheek.

Majesty and I had settled into our apartment. Life was getting better and better. Inevitably though, in all lives, trouble comes when you are calm and doing fine. I still had friends in the neighborhood where I grew up- not many- but a few, and we would go down to West Louisville to visit frequently.

One scorching hot summer day we were visiting a friend who had lived in my old neighborhood since I was a little girl. Ms. P was her name. She had become like a "street mother" to me over the years. Her house was very elegant, filled with beautiful plants, and trinkets, antique furniture and music always filled the house. People, young, old, crazy, and friendly, were always welcome at Ms. P's house. She was one of a kind, and she touched everyone's life in a special and unique way. This day we sat on her porch and I was listening to a message I had recorded on my handheld recorder a few days before. The words sang from the recorder relaying the goodness of Jesus Christ. I had two months, or so, prior accepted my calling into the ministry; with all of my flaws, vices, baggage and burdens. Three guys who grew up with me in the neighborhood some fifteen years before sat on the porch and combatively disputed the message I played from the recorder.

"You think you are better than me!" one yapped in agitation.

"How do you know God is real?" another questioned belligerently.

The third sat quietly as if he were contemplating on his reception of the message. He never said a word until I prepared to leave from the porch to go get some plastic for the driver's side window on my Mercury Topaz.

"Angel and Angel! Ms. P chanted. She was always hooking something or someone up for one reason or another. Angel had been the one who sat quietly contemplating. How ironic that our names matched. Being through all of the treacherous and failed relationships I had encountered in the past, I was just glad to have another opportunity to get to know someone new. He seemed like a nice guy, but I later found out that he had a plethora of baggage himself. Baby mama drama! Oh no! I'd never been one who ran towards drama, but this time I ran blindly into a chaotic dramatic situation. Angel and I dated, if you will, for a while, and we had fun when the mother of his children wasn't manipulating his mind or vice versa. Our kids played well together when they were around. When his kids weren't around he began to be very possessive. Sometimes I wanted to be with my friends; sometimes I just wanted it to be me and Majesty; sometimes I wanted it to be just me, without him. He didn't take too kindly to my "me time" and started sneaking around my apartment and following me to and from the complex. Sometimes I would just tolerate his unwanted company just to avoid the eerie feelings that came from sounds and shadows that showed up in my solitude. Strangely, they never occurred when he was right up under me.

As I endured this, yet another, abusive relationship, I thought back on the one I'd barely escaped from just one year prior.

In 2000 I worked for a friend of my father at his tax service. This particular March day was dreary and dank. I had had a long day at the office with Rico, Johnnie, and Charlie. Each one of us had our own personalities, but we got along pretty well considering. The whole day I had thought about going to Alabama in-between the scrambling of tax customers who ran in and out, back and forth to the office. When it was quitting time, I had a plan in my mind. I would go pick Majesty up from day care, go to the bank, go to the service station to have the car checked for traveling, and then we would hit the road to reach Gordo, Alabama. This is the small country town an old acquaintance of mine lived by now. Earlier that day in my thoughts I reviewed the continuous cycle I had been battling. It was a bad relationship, but somehow in my twisted mind I thought that Briant and I could repair and rekindle our relationship. As I drove up 264-East to pick Majesty up, I thought about the previous month. Briant lived in Louisville then. This male was a handsome one but his attitude didn't match his physical description. He'd been possessive and abusive- go figure. Nonetheless, even after our knock-down drag out altercation not thirty days before, I still consciously planned this trip. The altercation occurred after I had gone to spend some "girl time" with a friend who was dealing with some relationship issues herself. When I returned to my "boyfriend's" house, all hell broke loose! To make a long story short, he threw all of my belongings that were at his place (from when Majesty and I spent the night) over a second story banister into the slushy, dirty, melting snow. I had let him use one of my TVs which he also threw over the banister along with a VCR that shattered into pieces. Briant then picked up the body of the shattered VCR and aimed to throw it at my face. Thank God for reflexes! I turned sideways to avoid a smash to the face only to end up with a black, blue and green bruise right below my right shoulder. After this incident I was determined to get out of this cycle. Let me explain in a bit more depth. Even when these types of incidents would happen, I would somehow find a way to take the blame and attempt to fix the problem. I would always end up apologizing for being a punching bag, then crying and begging for him to talk to me. This happened in relationship after relationship. So I wondered to myself, still driving, on autopilot by now, "If this is the outcome every time and I say I have such strong determination to get out, why do I keep going back?"

I got off the expressway at Poplar Level Road and continued on my journey to Alabama. I stopped at each of my planned destinations and drove onto I-65 South at about 8:30pm. Briant met me at a gas station in Tuscaloosa, Alabama and greeted me with a kiss and a hug. We were all smiles... totally ignoring the last encounter we had, besides telephone conversations. Actually for the entire weekend I had no thoughts of the past, only hopes for the future. Of course, because nothing lasts forever, that ended. I had planned to leave for home on Monday afternoon, and on that day I was preparing to do so. The incident that occurred within an hour before my planned departure made me know that neither this trip nor this man belonged in my life.

Majesty had a can of barbeque Vienna sausages I

had given her for a snack. She had left two in the can sitting on the dresser. For some reason Briant wanted me to finish them off.

"HMMM." He shoved the Vienna sausage hanging from his mouth into my face as if he wanted me to bite the half from his lips. I said I didn't want any... Briant proceeded to forcefully shove the sausage towards my mouth... then aggressively he threatened me with a look that could kill. I took the bite only for him to open his mouth and the other half fall onto my white sweatshirt. Naturally I reacted. "Uuuuggghhh!" as I immediately grabbed one of Majesty's baby wipes to clean it off.

"Did I do that on purpose?!" Briant shouted angrily. "What is wrong with you?" he yelled in escalating rage.

I was confused at the sudden anger, but I continued packing our things to leave. Within a split second, after trying to ignore the derogatory comments, I felt my head catch up with my body as he yanked me towards him by the collar of my shirt. At first, I didn't realize that it was as serious as it was until I laid eyes on Briant's contorted expression. Then I was terrified! A perfect weekend had turned instantly into a nightmare come true! For the next hour I was being smacked, choked, punched, kicked and spit on. Every time I tried to escape he would knock me down or jerk me by my hair. The last time I tried to run, before I was finally rescued by one of his older cousins, he pulled me back and locked the bedroom door. He smacked me numerous times and even attempted to bash me over the head with a glass vase. Thank God for chandeliers! As Briant pulled the vase from over his head preparing for a blow to my head, the pursuit was intercepted by the light fixture hanging from the ceiling. He dropped the vase and used the forceful rage to knock me down to my knees. All I could do was pray! As I pleaded to God to save me from this destruction, Briant struck me on the side of my head with an open palm and then punched my head with a closed fist.

"Shut up! Listen to me! Talk to me!" he demanded with another three strikes.

I did not stop praying because, at that point, I knew that the only one I could depend on to save me was God, considering that there were three people right down the hall in the living room with Majesty. I knew that they had heard my curdling cries and screams for help. No one came... I was elated in the midst of my fear that my daughter was on the outside of the door; at least she wasn't watching what she was hearing.

Right before the rescuer came to the bedroom door,

Briant had choked me for the third time. This time it had
been longer than the other two. He threw me on the bed and
gripped my neck with a grip of death. He looked me
straight in my eyes and glared at me struggling for my
breath and my life.

"You are not gonna make it this time bitch! You are
gonna die!" he threatened me convincingly and with no
remorse.

Less than twenty-four hours passed and Majesty
and I were back on the highway headed home, by the Grace
of God!!!

Would this "Angel" currently in my life become
another "Angel of death"? Only time would tell. As for
now, 2002, life was going on.
My son was born and he was not fathered by Angel. Go
figure…

For the next few years I went through the motions
of living. I tried to take care of my two children- with
prospects of companions and hopeful father figures moving
in and out of our lives. Needless to say that neither of their
daddies were there to be the head of the household. So I
searched and searched, to no avail, to find someone to share
this heavy load I had accumulated in life up to this point.
All I wanted was the fairy tale to come true- the one I'd

dreamt of all of my childhood, youth and young adulthood (which, by now, I'd learned, but not yet accepted, would not become my life). I wanted to be the wife and mother in a two-parent family that lived happily ever after... but OOOH! The pursuit of happiness...

Angel Marie Renee' Mayes

Chapter 14
The Word of My Testimony

"You prepare a table before me in the presence of my enemies; You anoint my head with oil;"   *Psalm 23:5b NKJV*

"Snap out of it! Be released! Come out of the pit!" I heard a still small voice continue to speak to my soul. I had wallowed in the slimy pit of the negative things that had happened to me for so long, I didn't allow the gifts I had been so graciously given to flourish. I had let the mundane mountain of molestation stand in my way for so long I had forgotten that I had the power to speak to the mountains, with the faith of a mustard seed, and they would have to move. I had allowed the pitiful pit of promiscuity to swallow me up just like the whale had done Jonah. Running away from the pain and confusion of being sexually abused, I ran directly into sexual, mental, and emotional abuse. I would sabotage every relationship because, subconsciously, I awaited the other party to do something wrong or to ignore me. I'd lost myself. I'd become co-dependent on anyone and anything available. The word of God says that, in order for us to be delivered out of bondage (which I was trapped in unwillingly yet nonchalantly) and to overcome the heaviness of the burden is to confess our sins one to another. I have pondered and dwelled on my downfalls for far too long- and I must now celebrate ME! I must now celebrate the "ME" I have grown to be; the mother, sister, friend, and cousin; the wonderful, loving, compassionate, talented, ambitious, intelligent, and strong young woman of God I have become! Now I will embark upon a platform of peace and tranquility using all experiences of life as stepping stones to a new and better realm of life in the Spirit of God, the body of Christ. In Romans 8:28, I believe Paul means For (now) we know, that all things work together for the good of them who love the Lord and who are called according to His purpose.

Now I want to break this down into bread crumbs as we eat the Word of Life- starting with "NOW". Now, meaning "at present time; immediately; given current situation; or up to present time". So Paul writes "For now…" I do not believe that he means for "only this moment", but "Because now…" Because now- even after trials, tribulations, abandonment and abuse, bumps on the head and falls on the face, we know… "We know"; we hold information in mind; we are certain about something; we realize something; we comprehend something. So again, "Because now we know that all things" All, meaning everyone or everything; the whole of… all things work together." Working together meaning interacting with others for a purposeful effort or function. So once again "Because now we know that all things work together…" Because immediately, at present time, we are certain about or realize that everything and everyone interacts with each other for a purposeful effort…Now we move on to the purpose…the good! The Good! The good of them who love the LORD! The Lord being Jesus Christ our Lord and Savior! I love the Lord because HE first loved me! He kept me… through every situation I mentioned along with others that were not mentioned, but just imagine… Beyond sodomy… and mental anguish… like the woman with the issue of blood in Mark 5:25-34... I had tried everything I knew to be set free from this cyclic spiral. I met Jesus in the midst of it all, and He held me close so I wouldn't let go. So from here we will enter into a new realm of "My Story" which I have been purposefully called to share.

Angel Marie Renee' Mayes

Chapter 15
Healed

"My cup runs over." Psalm 23:5b NKJV

(The following is a personal piece of freelance poetry that expresses my personal experience with being healed from brokenness.)

As a broken vessel kneeling over in a fetal position.
Trying and attempting to come into a liberated state.
Not complaining, for I am still in being, but beginning to see and know that there is much more.
Many more places for me to grace with that greatness which is embedded within me.
Lacking the sight to feel my way through, by the directive instructions by which I
have been immobilized in order, step by step…
to breath in the aroma, to taste the words which fall off of my lips and into the laps, ladles and larynxes of those who will choose to listen.
This is calling on my life.
To experience and conquer laceration to the soul, malediction of the mind, a muzzled, mutilated spirit caused by the tug of war inside and outside of this broken, crumbling vessel.
Only to succumb to the mighty will and become liberated through
the power of the Most High and Holy GOD.
The potter takes my lacerated soul and stitches it sufficiently
to be submerged in HIS purpose.
He then marinates my mind in adaptive assurance, so that HIS mind will remain in me.
He frees the bondage within and caresses every morsel of

mutilation, providing healing.
So now this vessel has been repaired beyond breakability.
Standing strong and submerged in the Holy Spirit of the
Heavenly Healer.

Oh! If you didn't already know, God blessed me with the gift to write poems. This one is one of my very favorites. I reveal a lot of deep, up close and personal experiences in my poems if you can feel, taste, see, hear and smell where I'm coming from. This poem speaks to my "illnesses", weaknesses, issues and thorns in my side and how God Almighty delivered me from mental bondage. As I lean on His Everlasting Arms and rest in His Safety (Psalm 91), I am gradually- bit by bit, slowly but surely and by and by- healed from the inside out. I now understand that we will understand HIM better by and by, and the sweet by and bys are wonderful! It's kind of like hind-sight being always 20/20! When we are in a hurting situation or a hurling circumstance, we don't get it. We have no idea; although we long to be free and strive to be liberated, why we are in this position in life? For instance, why did I go through the pit of promiscuity? Well, while engulfed in the pit, I did not get it... The after-effects of constantly failed, abusive or confused relationships would begin to pull me to look for a way out, which I never did find, neither do I now, immediately. But in the sweet by and by... If you know the levels of by and bys you are surely shouting and dancing right now! The Lord said in His Word that we would understand Him better by and by, meaning as we go, little by little, bit by bit and from the inside out! Yes Lord! Halleluiah!

As we go on this part of the journey, realize that we are going together for the first time. I've never been down this part of the road. Right now, I'm walking by faith and believing that all things truly do work together for the good of them who love the LORD!

The Lord catapulted me into this sharing experience, so I'm right with you on what to expect next. Well, my best sister and I always say, "Expect the unexpected...!" So here we go...

What is in need of healing? Or would we ask, "Who is in need of healing?" First and foremost, we must understand what "heal" means. To cure, to restore to health, to make well, to mend, to settle, to reconcile, to rebuild. When contemplating all of these definitions of "heal", what initially comes to mind? A wound? A sore? Something that hurts or is painful? Now we must look around the complete umbrella of concepts in this idea of "something". Something could be a tangible or intangible thing. I remember once in Lexington, my cousins and I were racing across the front yard. "On your mark, get set…" a family member shouted. In hearing those words I prepared myself to win the race. Mentally, I got on my mark and set my mind to win. "Go!" The commencement for the race was complete. We all took off to reach the finish line. Halfway to the mark… my right foot stepped right down into a small ditch in the grass, causing me to lose footing and fall knee first onto the concrete walkway between the yards. It felt like I slid for about a mile! In hind-sight, I believe the imagined length of the slide was actually embarrassment hovering over me. I felt hot all over. When I stood up I looked at my knee only to see a large portion of my skin removed and replaced by a patch of white. The first thing I thought was, "Oh my gosh! I hurt my knee down to the meat!" Then the blood began to flow. Do you see and feel the irony in this?!(Fall- hurt- white- blood flows!) This wound was a tangible thing. I could literally see and feel the pain! Then I think of a time when I had been in the pit of promiscuity. Oh what a pit! Many times I felt heartbreak… my heart hurt… I was internally bleeding! A few times I had abortions and felt the pain of grief and shame. These were intangible. I would say, in hind sight, or in a by and by, that the intangible hurts were the most painful.

The wound on my knee healed. First there was a wet, bloody, open wound on my knee. But in approximately a week and a half, it had been nursed, carefully handled, mended, and restored to health. My knee was healed, although there was a faint scar left there. The best thing about that was that I did not feel the pain that I felt during the healing process! Now the intangible pain has been a different process. The pain that these kinds of wounds brought was not so easily nursed or healed. Intangible means that one cannot literally touch the subject. The pain from a broken heart was not one on which alcohol or peroxide could be poured to start the healing process. It was not a pain which was visible to the physical eye. The same would go for grief and shame. There had to be an intangible method to nurse, cure, and rebuild intangible wounds. One might wonder where intangible methods could be found. As I prayed for the restoration of the intangible wounds on the inside of me, the Lord began to show me that having sex or masturbation (tangible), drinking alcohol or smoking weed (tangible), searching for satisfaction in companionships (tangible) were not sufficient healing methods for intangible wounds. In 2 Corinthians 10:4 the Word of God tells us that the weapons of our warfare are not carnal, but mighty through God to the pulling down of strongholds. Carnal and tangible would be synonymous in the subject matter at hand. Carnal means relating to one's physical needs or appetites (tangible). So we must understand that the inner wounds- that we cannot see or literally touch- require supernatural (intangible) healing methods. Now we must search for the intangible methods to begin the restoration and rebuilding process. I walk back down the road to the beginning where the wounds began to appear...

Chapter 16
I Touched the Hem

When I reached the beginning of the journey, in the intangible state, I began to gather up all of my wounds. I had been like the woman with the issue of blood. For twelve long years she had a hemorrhage from her vagina. It was as if she was constantly on her menstrual cycle for twelve years. She had tried everything she knew to rid herself of this disturbing hemorrhage.

For over twelve and even over the eighteen years the infirm woman suffered from illness (Luke 13:10-17), I had suffered from issues of bloody wounds and could not raise myself up from mundane places; from stagnancy; from depression; from unresolved issues; from un-forgiveness; from sadness... I felt kind of like Job when he had all of the boils covering his body- only mine were invisible and intangible.

I entered into the supernatural realm of healing and found that there are various ointments for intangible wounds. Now was the time to sort through the types of wounds and search for the proper healing methods. This process would be similar to going into Walgreens and searching the aisles for medications for specific symptoms. If your stomach was upset you would search for medications to settle your stomach. If you had a migraine headache you would search for pain relievers. If you had a cut on your hand you would search for antibiotic ointment and band aids.

The first wound I focused on was abandonment-feeling abruptly left... as if no one genuinely cared for me, or feeling worthless and lost. On my first visit to the physician I learned, in Luke 11:9, that if I sought, in Christ, for whatever I was in need of that I would find it. So I sought for love and care. The physician gave me two prescriptions. One was for John 3:16 where God loved the world so much that He gave His only begotten Son to give me eternal life! The second prescription was for I Peter 5:7 where Peter directed me to cast all of my cares upon the Lord, because He cares for me! I applied these methods to the wound of abandonment, and sooner than later I was comfortable enough to leave the band-aid off and watch the wound close up. What an amazing form of healing!

In continuing to search for more healing, I found that it was more painful than just covering up the wounds with band-aids. When I peered deeper and further down the road, many times I wanted to turn back. When I applied the prescription for love, there seemed to come more heartache and bleeding. The still small voice continued to speak to my heart, the intangible one, and directed me to keep pressing forward. Weeping may endure for a night but JOY will come in the morning...

I found myself weeping more frequently than ever as I applied the first two prescriptions for love and care. I relived, in my mind, the time the guy in Alabama tried to kill me after he'd promised that he loved me so much. I reminisced on the time Shon made me put his penis in my mouth on the side of my cousin's house... When he sicced the big black and brown dog on me for not opening my legs... when he held a car jack over his shoulder as if to prepare to hit me with it, and I cringed at the thoughts of the stalker lurking... And I wept and wept...

When the realization of "abiding in the Lord" settled inside of my heart, I then understood that each time I revisited those horrifying experiences without applying the intangible, spiritual prescriptions, I was causing the wounds to be opened right back up as if they were freshly made. I learned that anger and disgust, or vengeance and malice were not the correct weapons for this warfare. I had to abide, which means to dwell and to await and/or withstand something. So when I experienced something or thought about something that rekindled these memories, which brought many others tagging along, I had to apply the prescriptions and wait for the healing while enduring the pressure, the pulling, the oozing and the drying up of the wound. If I didn't allow the complete process of healing to take place, the wounds would constantly be reopened. Please believe that this obedience did not come quickly or easily for such a stubborn hard-head as myself. Wow! I know I've been changed! I never before would have admitted that I am stubborn or hard-headed! Well I must thank God Almighty for this growth through yet another process of healing!

Returning to the lives of the woman with the issue of blood and the infirm woman, I must compare myself in various ways to them. They had suffered for a lengthy amount of time and this had to have been a great hindrance to their lives. Whether they knew what to do, or just couldn't do it for whatever reason or reasons there might have been, I can and will speak for them as a woman and say that they must have longed for freedom from these debilitating conditions. Just as I suffered for many years (and I'm still being healed), these two women suffered terribly. Not until they got to Jesus were they healed. They may have heard about Him or even known who He was, but not until the one touched the hem of His garment, and the other was touched by Jesus at the synagogue were either of them healed.

So my true healing began when I gave my wounds over to Jesus. As I use the intangible methods in the Word of God and apply the proper prescriptions, I reach another "by and by" and "bit by bit". I still have many open wounds and still have quite a few in process of being healed, but I have touched the hem of His garment and he is making me whole!

"Surely goodness and mercy shall follow me all the days of my life; and I will dwell in the house of the Lord forever!" <u>Psalm 23:6 NKJV</u>

To be continued...

Made in the USA
Columbia, SC
08 October 2022

68897474R00070